Dedicated to our daughter Ellya Fa'atoese Miracle
You are Precious, Beautiful, and God Sent ♡

Toe nonofo i le fale? O le a le Koronavairusi? (Stay home again? What is Coronavirus?)
(A book about a child's curiosity about the Covid-19 Pandemic)
Copyright © 2021 by: Princess Mariana Publishers
All rights reserved. No part of this book may be reproduced
in any manner whatsoever without written permission of the
author and publisher. Except in the case of brief quotations
and reviews. Thank you for your support and for
buying an authorised edition. For more information, pls.
Contact: #VaoeseLimutauKava :
on Facebook & Instagram
Written By: Vaoese Kava
Illustrations By: Sofiia Butusova
ISBN 978-0-6450030-7-9 (hardcover)
ISBN 978-0-6450030-9-3 (paperback)
ISBN 978-0-6450030-8-6 (eBook)
Distributed Worldwide
First Edition Mar. 2021

Disclaimer:
This book is not meant to be used, nor should it be used, to diagnose or treat
any medical condition. For diagnosis or treatment of any medical problem, consult
your own physician. The publisher and author are not responsible and are not
liable for any damages or negative consequences from any treatment, action,
application or preparation, to any person reading or following the information
in this book. This story is fictious and provides limited information and do not constitute
endorsement of any websites or other sources. Readers and their families/friends should
consult their own doctors/physicians for any medical issues.

Tinā/Mother:

"Nive, na 'e fa'alogo i le upu Koronavairusi, lea e talanoa so'o ai tagata o le TV male Leitio"?

Nive, Did you hear the word Coronavirus, also mentioned on TV and the Radio"?

Nive:
"Ioe tina, ua ou fa'alogo i le upu lea. O le a le uiga o le Korona-vairusi"?

Yes mother, I've heard that word mentioned many times. What is Corona-Virus?

Tinā/Mother:
"O le vairusi o se siama la'ititi e faigata na va'aia e mata".

A virus is a tiny germ that is not easily seen with our eyes

Tinā/Mother:

"O vairusi fo'i ia e faigofie ga lele 'i le 'ea, ma pipi'i i so'o se mea, e pei o ou lima ma isi vaega o lou tino".

This virus is very small and can easily be airborne and stick to many things, like your hands and other parts of your body.

Tinā/Mother:
"E mafai na pipi'i 'i laulau ma nofoa, faitoto'a ma isi mea".

They can easily stick to tables, chairs, doors and other things

Tinā/Mother:

"A o'o i totonu o lou tino, e faigofie ona toe fa'ateleina atu nisi vairusi ma mafai ai na 'e ma'i".

If these germs travel inside your body, it will be easy for them to make more germs and you could get very sick

"E tatau ga 'e fa'aitete ma 'ia 'aua ne'i o'o le siama lea i totonu o lou tino".

You should be very careful that this germ doesn't enter inside your body

Nive,

"E iai ni siama i totonu 'o lo'u tino i le taimi nei"?
Do I have germs inside my body right now?

Tinā/Mother:

"Ioe, ae 'o siama ia 'e le malolosi".
Yes, but those germs are not very strong

"O le karonavairusi lea ua pipisi i le tausaga 2020/2021, e malosi tele, 'A 'e a'afia ai, e mafai na 'e ma'i 'i le Koviti-19".
The Coronavirus that is spreading now in 2020/2021 is a bad germ, and if you catch it, you can get Covid-19

Tinā/Mother:

O le Koviti-19 e faigata tele, e mafai ona a'afia ai ou mamā ma faigata ai lau manava.

Covid-19 could damage your lungs and you could find it hard to breath

Nive:

Tinā, o le a la ni mea e tatau ona ou faia ina ia 'aua ne'i maua ai a'u i le Koviti-19?

Mother, What can I do to avoid catching Covid-19?

Tinā/Mother:
"E mafai na mama'i tigaina isi, pe oti fo'i. E fa'aitete fo'i tatou mo tagata matutua, ma e ua maua i fa'ama'i faigata e pei o le Kanesa, Suka, ma'i o le Mama po'o le fatu".

But some of us can get very ill and could lead to death. We should be careful around the elderly, and those with health problems like cancer, diabetes, lung and heart disease

Tinā/Mother:

"Mo le saogalemu o tagata uma, e lelei le fai 'o mea nei".
1. E sili atu le nonofo i le fale e saogalemu a'o pesi le fa'ama'i.
2. Fa'aoga telefoni fe'avea'i ma le initaneti/telefoni fa'aVitio e talanoa ai i tagata o lou aiga e nonofo mamao ma 'oe,

For the safety of ourselves and others, we should consider the following:
1. Stay home if you can,
2. Use mobile phones and the internet/zoom calls to talk with loved ones who are far from you.

About the Author:

Vaoese Kava "aka" Ese Limutau Noa Aiono has always had a passion for writing since she was a young girl. This later inspired her to study Arts and Business. She completed her Business Administration studies, earning her MBA from the Australian Institute of Business, South Australia. She's a wife, a mother, and a grandmother to the adorable Amulek & Evalyn.

Due to covid-19 with its many restrictions and precautions worldwide, she's decided for the benefit of her young audience, to put in writing/illustrations, her twist on the Coronavirus Pandemic and give the experience from her perspective as discussed with her only daughter Ellya, pictured here. Follow her on Instagram & Facebook #VaoeseLimutauKava

I Love You

PRINCESS
MARIANA
PUBLISHING